STEP

The Day I Told Myself

"Enough Is Enough"

TERESA A. STITH

STEP

ISBN-13: 978-1-7332744-0-1

ISBN-10: 1-7332744-0-5

Publisher- A Faith That Works Publishing

Website: afaiththatworks.com

STEP

The Day I Told Myself "Enough is Enough"

One of the worst things that you can do

to yourself

is to have a vision for your life

and allow fear or feelings of inadequacy

to stop you from pursuing your dreams

Enough is Enough!

STEP

DEDICATION

This book is dedicated to yours truly for daring to step outside of myself and reach for the greater that I so desperately wanted for my life. I knew that God had an awesome plan already laid out and awaiting me, but I needed the reassurance that because it was mine, I could just reach up and grab it. It was easier said than done, I thought. Up to this point, I had not been physically satisfied with the way that things have played out in my life, however, I have learned that "in whatsoever state I am in" I will therewith be content (Philippians 4:11). There were times that I literally forced myself to be content because I did not want to face the fear of failing, if I stepped out. There were other times that I would step out and then quickly retreat back to a place that was familiar to me because I did not understand how to sustain myself in the step. I've learned that each step that you will take in life must be taken in faith! You're either going to trust God in it or not. The Bible tells us "Now the just shall live by faith: but if any man draw back, my soul shall have no pleasure in him (Hebrews 10:38). Fear has claimed a lot of people's destinies simply because they were not brave enough to STEP forward into newness or purpose. They lacked the faith that God required them to have due to them not being able to see the vision for themselves. There will be times that although you won't see your path plainly, a STEP is still required. Sometimes the Holy Spirit pulls and tugs at our hearts trying to get us to take that step, but fear arrests our faith and we begin to question if it was actually God speaking to us, or something that we have told ourselves to do because of a current situation. I know this all too well because I had a similar experience. I had become so frustrated and overwhelmed on my job (at the time) with the staff that I supervised and the overall daily operations of the facility that I began to pray that God would deliver me from the place. As time went on, I forgot what I had asked God for and was rather perplexed as I sit in my office one night and I hear a voice telling me to leave. I knew that I was the only one in the area at the time, but I slowly left my work area to step across the hall to make sure no one was in the area talking to me. No one was there. As I sit back down at my desk to begin my work again, I hear the voice a second time saying "I told you to leave." This time, being sure that it was the Lord, I put down my pen, looked up to Heaven and I said, "okay Lord, I'll do it." I took no thought about what I was doing, and the very next day I came in to work early enough to catch the Human Resource office open, and I submitted my two-weeks' notice. It did not ever occur to me what I had done until after I had already left my job. I began to cry, scream, pace the floor, cry some more, pray, scream, cry…what had I done! I went back and replayed the whole scenario with the voice telling me to leave and everything. I KNEW it was God, I KNEW it, but what I did not understand was why?...why had He told me to leave my job?...what was I supposed to be doing? My mind began to play tricks on me. I began to consider that I was almost 20 years on my job, so close to retirement and I gave it all up. Was that really God? Had I made a mistake? I began to question myself. I shared what happened with a couple of my Sisters from the church and felt like they did not believe me either. I felt like they even questioned…why would God tell me to leave my job like that? I had a new car, and bills like everyone else. I had no additional income coming in so why would God say that? I did not understand it either and as bad as I felt after talking to my Sisters, I held fast to what I believed that God had said to me. As I began to quiet myself before the Lord, after almost crying myself to death, God began to speak to me again. I had cried so much on this particular day that I decided to lie down and take a nap. As I lay on my bed looking up at the ceiling and drifting off to sleep, I heard the Spirit say "A Faith That Works." I repeated "A Faith That Works," "what's that?" I asked. The Lord went on to say that it would be worldwide. Then I began to see a website, writing, etc. I sit up in my bed and as I began to speak those things that the Spirit was speaking to me, it all began to come together. I Googled how to do my own website, I created a page on Facebook, I began to share my stories and testimonies through personal blogs on my website, etc. People from all over the world began to tap into "A Faith That Works." Before I knew it, God was giving me a book. I had no clue whatsoever that I would be writing a book about anything. I didn't even know I had a book in me, never considered it...BUT GOD! Because I dared to STEP out on what God was telling me to do, not considering what I would lose for myself, God has blessed me tremendously! This is my fourth published work. So you see, your faith has to be greater than your fear! DARE to step out and trust God. He alone holds our future and **only** responds to our faith!

Right now I want you to repeat after me…say "I am worthy, I am qualified, and I will STEP!" Stop listening to the lies of the devil! You deserve all that God has for you. Let Him help you to birth your purpose. Listen, usually when you know that you have an enemy, you try to avoid them by staying out of their way (if you're smart). Nobody wants to deal with the trouble associated with the drama that someone who doesn't like you can bring. But the day will come that it will be much easier to face your enemies and seek to resolve the issues, so that you can both move forward. Well, the day that I decided that I would face this enemy, was the same day that my life began to change. See, fear caused me to be stagnant in my spiritual and physical growth. It made me second guess my abilities and it challenged my character. It made me question my own faith at times, and made me believe that I was not intelligent enough to succeed. It made me feel inadequate and worthless. I thought that I would always be a person who would struggle for everything that I wanted in life. In an effort to prove fear and the devil wrong, I made hasty decisions and suffered the consequences for having done so. Listen, my dear brothers and sisters: Has not God chosen those who are poor in the eyes of the world to be rich in faith and to inherit the kingdom He promised those who love Him? (James 2: 5). I declare to you today that you are RICH in Christ Jesus because of the redemptive work that He did at Calvary by shedding His blood on the cross for your sins. You are smart enough, you are classy enough, and you are more than capable of doing whatever you have purposed in your mind to do. Don't let fear be the reason you stop trying. Don't let fear cause you to give up. Choose right now to STEP into your next level of living! On this level of living there is no more lack! There is no more paycheck to paycheck scrambling because you have been equipped with everything that you need to be successful and productive in life. I told fear that its reign in my life was over and that I will now walk in NEWNESS! See, I had to get rid of the slave mentality that I was carrying around, always feeling sorry for myself. I had to tell myself "yeah you went through what you went through to get to where you needed to get to BUT…those days of suffering are over!" There's no sense in going through if you're not going to learn "why" you went through in the first place. I will tell you that a lot of it was poor planning or not planning at all. Still some of it was not being accountable or taking responsibility for my actions. Yet the bulk of it was simply DISOBEDIENCE! We always think that we know what's best for our lives, but I will be the very first to tell you that I could have saved my own self some headache and heartache had I only obeyed the instructions that were given to me so long ago to simply "wait" on the Lord. Here I am now, ripe and ready and just now learning how to "let go and let God" have His way!

I've learned that I have been keeping my own self in bondage by failing to step out on faith and believe that God's got me no matter what. Sure we may suffer loss, and when we consider that we may lose something that may be of value to us, we reconsider the

STEP and resort back to our own little corners in our homes and live our lives with regret. You have got to be bigger than what you can physically see!

S T E P !!!

I allow myself to set healthy boundaries.

To say no to what does not align with

my values,

To say yes to what does.

Boundaries assist me to remain healthy,

honest,

and living a life that is true to me

Minus the Fear!

-Lee Horbachewski

TABLE OF CONTENTS

STEP
INTO
YOUR
NEXT
SEASON

The Process

I

The whole process of stepping involves YOU taking one foot and confidently placing it in front of the other as you move your body as a unit, forward. Stepping does not only involve your feet, it involves your mind. You cannot do one without the other. Your mind tells your body how it ought to behave, so our actions are somewhat controlled by the way in which we think. I know this all too well because there were times that I literally struggled with doubt and unbelief. Because I was not thinking right, things in my life was out of sync. There was no order and definitely not any structure. The old people used to say, "when it rains, it pours" humph…I gave raining and pouring a whole new meaning! There was more chaos going on in my life than I had time to deal with and this cycle continued until I began to change the way that I thought about it. When my *thinking* changed, the way that I dealt with the chaos changed. What I found was that as I began to consider each thing that was wrong in my life, how to deal with it became clear. I had to look at it. My Pastor always reminds us to "nip things in the bud" this simply means to kill it at the root. There are things in our lives that we have become accustomed to just sweeping underneath the rug, but given the right situation at the right time, has the potential to cause a great fire in our lives because of the residue that we've allowed to linger on in our hearts and in our minds. So this process of stepping involves you daring to go back and look at some things and kill it at the root. It could be something that someone said to you

15 years ago, if you are still traumatized by it,
call it out. Challenge it, give it no more place in
your life, nip it in the bud and move forward.
As you do this remember, it is not just about
how *you* feel, you must be willing to consider
the other person's feelings as well and be able
to come to a mutual resolve. Go into this thing
looking for a solution, not justification and be
free in your stepping.

Working in a correctional facility for the
last 20 or so years, has allowed me the
opportunity to talk with many of the offenders
and staff about looking at things in their lives a
little differently. When you are hurt by
someone, the only thing that you see
sometimes is how *you* were hurt, and not the
place of pain that the other person was in
when the statement was made. Many of those
that I've talked with either replaced the pain

with something else (drugs, alcohol, women, etc) or committed criminal acts against the violators. While many said that if they could go back and change the circumstances or the way in which they handled it, they would... there were many others who said given the opportunity, they would do it all over again. What's the difference? The difference is in *wanting* to do it. The difference is in wanting to look at it to come to a mutual resolve or *choosing* not to look at it because for you, this may be your power. You may feel justified, but justification does not make a thing right. Justification only provides you with another excuse to not look at your issues more in depth. To step, you must be willing to do this.

The process of stepping also involves your ability to think and believe that as you move, things will begin to shift and come together for the good of what you are seeking. Again, before you can get your feet to do anything, your heart and mind have already considered and weighed the obstacles that may come, but have decided that despite them, STEPPING is the best alternative. Regardless of what you may see with your physical eyes as you step, you must be willing to only focus on where you are headed and keep your mind set on accomplishing it.

"I have observed something else under the sun.

The fastest runner

doesn't always win the race,

and the strongest warrior

doesn't always win the battle.

The wise sometimes go hungry,

and the skillful are not necessarily wealthy.

And those who are educated

don't always lead successful lives.

It is all decided by chance, by being

in the right place at the right time"

(Ecclesiastes 9:11, NIV)

One thing that I love about this passage is that each one of these people STEPPED! Although the fastest runner expects to win, he oftentimes does not, but he keeps running. The strongest warrior doesn't always win, but he keeps fighting. The wise go hungry, the skillful is not wealthy, and the educated one is not always successful but each one of them has taken the steps necessary to fulfill his or her destiny. Have you?

The whole process of stepping will not be comfortable and it is not meant to be. If anyone who has made it to the top and told you that it was a breeze, has simply lied to you. Like anything else, the journey to success, wealth or any other thing that you set out to do is never easy simply because you have to face a lot of stumbling blocks, hindrances, and overcome some obstacles. One of the biggest challenges that you will ever have to face, will be YOU! First of all, you will have to deal with the fear that "you may not be able to do what you have set out to do." Erase this thought from your mind and replace it with the attitude and the confidence that "it WILL work." All too often we have allowed ourselves to discourage our own hearts by thinking that we are not ready or are undeserving of what we desire. Start feeding yourself some faith. Every time a negative thought rise up in your head, hew it down with something positive, this is how you build your confidence. Stop accepting lies from the devil. God made you a WINNER, so go out there and WIN! Be mindful while you are stepping that you will wrestle against things that you have had control over all of your life. To be successful, may mean relinquishing that control to someone better suitable to work the plan and who knows what they are doing. For the first year or so, after writing my first book, the sales on Amazon was so slow, it was ridiculous. I often wondered if I was doing something wrong, or not doing everything right. I did not trust people to help me because I just simply did not know who I could trust. One day the Lord spoke to me and said, "you have got to let people help you." God would connect me to people, but I was always skeptical about whether or not it was God or myself. I second guessed myself a lot because I did not want to offend God, and I did not want to overstep Him either. Because God knew my heart, I had to trust that He would also provide and take care of me. Clearly, I did not know what I was doing, so God had to connect me to someone already skilled in the thing that I was needing help with. Where it may have been hard for you to trust others, you will find yourself having to let your guard down a little and trust some people. You may lose some things so get ready. What I have learned during this process is that the ending of a thing is only the beginning of a greater thing. Lord knows, I have had to lose some stuff. It hurt me to my heart, but you cannot be so attached to stuff in this world, that you are not willing to sacrifice it for the greater good that is coming to you. You will get it back! Some things you may be better off without. When God began to put His purpose in me, some things I became glad to give away! I did not want anything to interfere with God's purpose for my life or the goals and visions I'd set for myself. You may shed some tears in this season and through this process, but be of good cheer, God knows what He is doing! Let Him work it! The process will consist of some stretching, purging, cleansing, and dying, but I promise you that when it is all said and done, you will emerge RIPE and READY lacking nothing! The Bible says "Beloved, I wish above all things that thou mayest prosper and be in health, even as thy soul prospereth" (3 John 1:2). See, this is not just about your pockets getting fatter, but about your Spirit prospering as well so...

Let God
S-T-R-E-T-C-H
you!

Train your mind to trust God's process of stretching. Let Him stretch you in your thinking, in your decision-making. The Lord urges us to acknowledge Him in all of our ways. We must train ourselves to depend on God, to ask His opinion or direction over our lives. We must equip ourselves to endure through stretching.

My Definition of Stretch...

1) To be **mentally and spiritually pulled** in a way that challenges your sanity but confirms your stance in the Lord.

2) Undergoing physical and mental anguish yet refusing to tear or break. To be extended beyond your normal ability to endure...

but you endure anyway.

The Stretching

II

Stretching became new to me here. I had never experienced suffering or molding to this extent and it was taking everything that I thought I knew about God and "going through" and it was calling me to answer!!! I remember this commercial that said "put your money where your mouth is" and while it was promoting toothpaste, this stretching process was promoting and producing faith and challenging me to either put up or shut up! I did not understand what was happening and "stretching" was the only way that I could describe this stage in my life to my friends and family. Unbeknownst to me, "stretching" actually did exist. I first got a whiff of it while watching a broadcast by Bishop T.D. Jakes and he was talking about being stretched. Prior to hearing this sermon, I thought stretching was something that I had come up with. The more that I tried to explain to people that I was being stretched, the more I thought I was losing my mind because people looked at me like "what is she talking about?" "What do you mean by stretching?" I didn't know what I meant, I only knew what was happening and I explained it as best I could.

So Bishop is talking about "stretching" and this stuck with me..."there are some things that God has for you and the only way that you are going to reach it is you have to stretch!" Stretching was challenging me mentally, I thought that if one more thing came to challenge me, that I would flip the switch and go crazy. I was being CRUSHED, PRESSED DOWN, and STRIPPED of my sanity it seemed, and one wrong move would send me packing to the nut house. I had sense enough though, to realize that I'd better stay right here and wait on the Lord. God was not speaking as fast as I thought He should and neither were my prayers being answered. More and more things came to challenge and test my faith. One mind told me to just fold and quit and the other kept saying hold on and trust God through the process. Which mind do you listen to? I chose the latter. I chose to trust God despite what I could see. It was like trials were coming out of nowhere to test my faith in God. Before I could consider one thing, something else was coming up against me. I started going through with my finances, my bills were jacked up, I could not get a handle on anything. My job was stressing me out. Everything that could have went wrong…did. I even had to give up one of my vehicles after the payments became more than I could handle AND I still had to go back into the field and teach FAITH to the people! I became so overwhelmed about my own situation and the struggling that I began to cry out to God "Lord help me, what is going on?" I began to tell God about all of the wonderful things that I thought I was doing to promote or advance the Kingdom, and how proud of me He should be. I told Him about the patience that He had given me and how I could see changes in my own life and I just kept finding things that I thought was good enough to persuade God to "send that relief" that I was asking for. My heart weeps as I consider that none of the things that I mentioned to God was what He was looking for from me in this season. He wanted OBEDIENCE! I hope this next phrase helps you, wherever you are on your spiritual journey.

You can work yourself to death to do what you think pleases God, and God will still be looking at that one thing that He asked you to do that you still have not done yet.

God does not get excited about STUFF! He gets excited about obedience. God needs people in this season who He can trust to do what He says. He needs people who are ready and not afraid to STEP! I kept putting off things that I knew that God was saying to do because I was afraid to step, I was afraid of what I might lose. I did not trust that God would be there to catch me if I fell. In all of my humanness, I had to ask God to forgive me. I'm so much more confident today than I was yesterday. Trusting God is a process, mainly because we have lived the bulk of our lives trusting in our own abilities. Oh, how vulnerable I felt when I had to relinquish that trust to someone else. I did not understand how to do that, but God taught me. He was there every step of the way, even when I could not see Him, He was watching.

During this stretching process, I became uncomfortable. I oftentimes imagined Jesus hanging there on the cross stretched from one end to the next. He was literally being PULLED apart, all for the glory of Him who called Him. I felt the pressure on my mental psyche as I too, was being separated from my flesh. I kept fighting to regain control over my thinking. I fought to bring and keep my mind under subjection to the Word of God as I battled situations and circumstances. God was pressing me. Like grapes going through a wine press, He was squeezing everything out of me that He knew that He had put in me. He was proving me, testing me to see if I would speak to these mountains or succumb to them. He was making me declare what the Word of God says and teaching me to stop looking at where I was and to only focus on WHO He was. Stop looking at what you're going through and focus on WHO is carrying you through it all. I kept telling myself that God is coming, He's going to show up any minute to this place and He's going to rescue me and set some things in order. I found every scripture that I could think of that made me believe that my suffering was not in vain, and when God still didn't come, my mind began to shift. I was literally losing it, I thought. Through all of this, God was still not responding. Can you imagine going through so much mental anguish and still be expected to perform normal in the real world and tell others to "have faith in God?" I think that it was *this part* that was causing me so much conflict. I was angry that God was applying all of this pressure on me inwardly and still expecting me to go out into the world and hold my chin up and smile. I was going crazy in my mind. I found myself again surrounded by darkness and battling depression and thoughts of suicide. I felt that God had abandoned me and was purposefully causing these things to happen. It's possible that, He was because I ASKED FOR THIS!

I will try to make this as clear as I possibly can. When you ask God for something, He does not forget what you asked Him for. See, I had been running my mouth and telling God "Lord, I want to be like You" "Lord, I want to know You in the fullness" "Lord teach me Your ways" "Lord, let me see what You see." All of these things I asked God

for and then forgot that I had asked. I can
laugh now, but it wasn't so funny when I was
going through. God taught me to stop asking
for things just to be asking, but BE READY to
go through to receive what I'm asking for. God
doesn't hold anything back from us.

Remember, if you ask Him for it, He's going to
condition you for it first...just don't forget that
YOU ASKED for it! God will STRETCH, PULL,
YANK, and SQUEEZE obedience out of you.
When He has a purpose or calling on your life,
you will obey!

ENDURE
YOUR
SEASON
OF
STRETCHING

Teresa A. Stith

The Purging

III

The next STEP is the process of purging. To be purged simply means "Lord, let me empty out myself so that You can fill me with more of Yourself. God cannot pour Himself into you when you choose to remain filled with a lot of other stuff. Remember, His Spirit cannot dwell in any unclean thing.

What? know ye not that your body is the temple of the Holy Ghost which is in you, which ye have of God, and ye are not your own? (1 Cor. 6:19)

During this stage in the process, I had to make some hard decisions. Hard, only because my flesh wanted to rebel. I had to come clean on some things that my flesh wanted me to tuck away or keep close enough for me to dip back into if needed. Purging means to get rid of, or remove, but I like the term "Drive out!"

See, I can't play with the devil. You either want

him gone or you don't. But to move forward in

your STEPPING, you need to kill some things

at the root! I can't wait for something to

happen to let that thing go, or someone to tell

me to let it go...*some things* I have to *drive out*

myself! You will know when you truly want to

get rid of something when you just do it!

Nothing out of the ordinary has to happen for

you to make the decision. If God told you to

leave that man or woman alone because they

were not right for you, could you do it? Why

does something have to happen to make us

obey what God already told us to do? Do what

God has said. Omg, I was good for this. I found

myself in an abusive relationship with a man

and nobody had to tell me that it was not good

for me to be there because I knew it. I wanted

to stay there and be with this guy only because he satisfied my flesh and my need for sexual gratification at the time. Every time I laid down with him, it seemed that the Holy Spirit was whispering for me to "get up." Although, I could hear and feel the Spirit's promptings, I could not pull myself up out of that situation. Then whenever we would have a disagreement, I would boldly profess, "that's why the Lord told me to leave you alone anyway!" (laugh out loud) I tell you the truth, we are some humorous creatures. I'm so thankful for grace and mercy, that God allowed me to live and mend my crooked ways. We should not take chances like this because one blow from the Lord and our lives could be over. Never take advantage of God's grace. God is faithful and just, and will show you who or what needs to be purged from your life. When He shows you, He will also show you how to remove them. Remember, it is not personal, God has a plan and purpose for our lives and it does not always include the people or things that we seem to attach ourselves to. When we grow in the Lord, our focus becomes strictly what His will is for our lives. God shows us how to love and who to allow in our space. Everyone won't fit and it's okay, just know that God has an ultimate plan for us from the time we were born until we leave this earth, and we have to subject ourselves and condition ourselves for the journey.

God has created us to love others and sometimes love causes us to disobey what God says. We do not want to hurt people's feelings, but we must remember that God can see more than we can. He knows the motives and intents of a man's heart. We do not always understand but sometimes our love for others prohibits them from seeing God for themselves. We can become stumbling blocks to others and not realize it. I had to learn a valuable lesson in this. Every time my kids called, I felt like I should be the one to run to their aid, despite God's pleas for me to separate myself from them. See, God wanted to be God to my children after all, I had prayed and asked Him to. Every chance I got, I was running to their rescue for every little thing, until one of my sons got incarcerated for committing a crime and spent time in prison. I had no choice then, but to trust God to keep Him. I could have avoided all of the heartache behind this, just doing what God had told me to do in the first place. I was right back asking God to forgive me again for being disobedient. One thing about the Lord, He is long-g-g-suffering. He will allow you to keep going around that same ole' mountain until you learn how to seek Him and acknowledge Him in all of your ways. Stop trying to do things without including God in it, because you will always have to go back and correct the error of your ways. So do it right the first time and save yourself the trouble.

I'm reminded of this ole' gospel hymn…

♫ ♫ ♫ ♫

Like the woman at the well I was seeking for
things that could not satisfy.
And then I heard my Savior speaking
"Draw from my well that never shall run dry"
Fill my cup Lord, I lift it up Lord,
come and quench this thirsting of my soul.
Bread of Heaven
feed me till I want no more.

STEP

Here's my cup,

fill it up

and make me whole.

Purge me with hyssop and I
shall be clean; wash me and I
shall be white as snow

Psa. 51:7

Teresa A. Stith

The Cleansing

IV

The cleansing part of the process is slightly different than that of the purging, but both are clearly essential to an effective STEP. *"When Jesus saw him lie, and knew that he had been now a long time in that case, he saith unto him, Wilt thou be made whole?" (John 5:6)* In other words, how long are you going to lie here? Do you want to be cleansed? Do you want to be made whole? Jesus already knew that the man was there because he wanted to be made whole, however, sometimes God needs to know that you are aware of just how much you need Him! He wants to hear just how bad you want your own healing. God has given us all a measure of faith. He wants to know that you have just enough hope and faith in your own self, that it will possibly move you from a *place of stagnation or waiting on others,* to where ever it may be that you are desiring to go. So STEP. In this season, you cannot wait on another person's opinion of what they think you should be doing. The only confirmation you need is that from God that it is your time to step. I had a terrible habit of second guessing myself and waiting on other people's approval before going forward into where I believed God was taking me. The years have passed me by, but thank God for a clear vision and clarity as I step. I have to constantly remind myself that I am not operating in my own strength, but in who I know that He is. Be reminded even as you step, that God has every resource that you need to fulfill His plans in your life.

Let's look at cleansing a little bit more in

depth. In the process of stepping, you want to be absolutely sure to rid yourself of any unforgiveness that you have tucked away in your heart. This is where you are called upon to be honest with yourself because to move forward and start anew, you have to be willing to deal with the stuff that other people cannot see, but that you are fully aware is happening. As God brings each thing back to your remembrance and you address them, you will see things gradually change and a shift taking place. This not only includes the way you talk, but also the way that you think. You will begin to become more aware of what you are saying and consider the impact that those words will have on your next move. Dr. Will Monroe said "Put a demand on your potential and tap into the genius on the inside of you." We get side-tracked looking at someone else's success and envying their ability to find their niche, instead of taking the time to discover our own. I used to get angry at myself when I would look and could not figure out what my purpose was. I often wondered if there was anything good in me. I wanted so desperately to be used by God and tried effortlessly to see any inkling of a gift that He had given me, that would assure me that I was one of His chosen ones. I'm sure glad that God did not base my abilities on what I thought of myself because back then, I felt worthless. Dr. Monroe taught me how to "give all of my energy to what I really wanted to do and surround myself with people who talk about plans, progress, and goals…not other people!" This is also how faith is built. Learn how to speak positive to the point that it becomes a habit, until you are absolutely convinced that what you are saying

is what Christ would say concerning you.
Believe on the promises of God. In Luke 6:45,
we read "The good man brings good things out
of the good stored up in his heart, and the evil
man brings evil things out of the evil that is
stored up in his heart. For out of the
abundance of the heart, the mouth speaks."
The whole process of cleansing allows you to
take the initiative to do away with all sin and
bitterness and reach out to someone for help.
When we confess our sins, God forgives our
sins and cleanse us from all unrighteousness.
The weight of sin and the guilt of sin is lifted
when we confess those sins to the Lord.

Wilt thou be made WHOLE?

To be cleansed means that you are choosing to submit yourself (all of you) to the Lord and turn away from anything else that tries to exalt itself above Him! This is a required STEP! You cannot step fully with a whole lot of baggage on you, get rid of that stuff. Listen, you must be fully committed to turning away from the world and turning towards God. As a matter of fact, the more sincere you are in turning towards the Lord, the more complete will be the turn! Let us pursue and chase after God and desire to be cleansed. "We will surely advance quicker by Divine guidance than we ever would by our own efforts" (Jeanne Marie Bouvie).

The Dying

V

What exactly does it mean to die? Did
you know that there is a value of and in dying?
You will not be able to live until you die!
Here's what I mean…the Spirit is indeed
willing, but the flesh is weak (Matthew
26:41). To completely STEP into your next
level, some dying is necessary. Dying is simply
choosing to give up all control over your life
and be totally led by the Spirit of God. When
you die, the Spirit controls your thoughts, your
actions, and motivates every decision that you
make. Dying takes place in your mind first,
because your steps are motivated by your
thinking. How you think will ultimately
dictate your behavior. The Word tells us to be
not conformed to this world, but transformed

by the renewing of our minds (Romans 12:2). You cannot have a new mind that is overwhelmed by old thoughts. There must be a shift in your thinking. There's nothing complicated about dying, you make a daily choice to follow hard after God, to listen to His voice and follow His leading. The more that you practice depending on Him, the easier it becomes to hear Him.

I recently shared with a coworker how, even at work, I have to be in tune with the Spirit of God. It can become pretty busy and the demands of the job can be overwhelming, but my focus and attention stays on the Lord, even in the midst of the chaos. He directs my paths and He's always reminding me of the next thing that I need to do. I trust Him. Because I have chosen to die to my own way of thinking, He has permission to disrupt my life at any time to ensure that I stay on the straight and narrow. When the Lord gives me instructions, I still have to choose to obey them. Obedience makes trusting God easier, and it makes dying obtainable. This is the value of death, when you can die and still live. This process of dying works in every stage of life. Your whole soul focus must be on what God has said, and what He is saying to you consistently. When He is not speaking, your ear should be just as inclined to hear than if He was speaking on a regular. We must practice hearing the Lord's voice to stay abreast of situations and events happening that may need to be covered in prayer prior to engaging.

The enemy has made it hard for us to die in this season by making all sorts of distractions that keep us so busy doing other things, that we are not paying attention to things that matter. Social media has become one of the biggest distractions in the history of mankind, used to consume all of our time and energy because we feel the urge to share with others, all about our day. How much time are we really spending with God? How much dying are we really doing during the course of the day? Also, I'm noticing more and more businesses are requiring employees to work on Sunday, a day that is clearly set aside for worship. Do you see how the enemy has blinded the hearts and minds of even some believers by using these worldly systems to distract us from trusting in the Most High God? We must as Jesus said in Matthew 26:41, "watch and pray."

For if you live according to
the flesh

you will die,

but if you put to death

the deeds of the body,

you will live.

For all who are led by the
Spirit of God are sons of
God"

(Romans 8:13-14).

To die for the child of God, means that you
choose every single moment of every single
day to stay awake, remain alert, pray without
ceasing (in the Spirit) watch, and listen for the
Spirit of God to move you and direct your

paths. We must start now to prepare ourselves for Heaven. How foolish it would be to wait until Christ returns to try to make preparations, when He has given us decades to get ready. Preparing to die does not mean that we cease to live. It means that we have made a conscious decision to walk in the integrity of who we are, by allowing the Holy Spirit to disrupt our flesh and arrest our wills, that God might be glorified in and through us. Remember, to perfect our step, we must include God in the step. Die!

The Stepping

VI

Are you ready to move into the next level of your Spiritual journey? Are you ready to move into the next level of your business? Here are a few more STEPS to ensure that you do so successfully.

S=**Speak**- Be careful what you are saying out of your mouth about your own business or whatever you are endeavoring to do in life. Words have power. If you want your audience to have faith in you, you must have faith in yourself. You must be just as persistent in those times that things are challenging, than in those when things are going well. People need to sometimes see how you handle the chaos and the success. This lets them know that they are dealing with a real individual and not someone who cannot identify with their struggles. Know your audience and allow your audience to know the real you. Nobody can share your story like you can. Going through the process and having the testimonials to back it up, makes the experience a bit more rewarding.

Also, be careful who you are speaking to about your business or your goals. Some people will act like they are all for you, but they are actually stealing your ideas and making your goals work for them. You may be wondering why things seem to be stagnant, and it's possible that it could be, because you have shared your vision out of season. It wasn't the right time to share it. Seal the deal first and then share it with others if you desire to do so.

T = **Think-** or rethink the goals that

you have set for yourself. Are they even obtainable? Be specific about what it is that you want, and be honest with yourself about your ability to accomplish your goals. Then, start taking the STEPS necessary to get there. Stop saying what you think, and think about what you are saying that will have an impact on your next move! Again, words have power. Out of the same mouth flows blessings and curses. You can't speak life one minute and death, doubt, and unbelief the next, and expect a fruitful harvest. You will have exactly what you say you will have! So think before you speak.

E= **Execute**- It is time to put your plan into action. What are you waiting for? You have talked about your plans, you have written them down, you may have even written books about it, but why is it that you still have not executed the plan yet? Is it fear? Is it finances? What is it? In this season, you're going to have to utilize faith to get you to your next level. This is your ACTION year and you have got to be ready to STEP! Time is of the essence. Nobody has it all the way together, it's in your stepping that you will learn what you need to do to perform at a higher level. You're not going to learn what to do until you step out to do that thing. Sometimes you may need to fall. Falling, or failing teaches us how to rework and improve ourselves to be better. It also teaches us not to be afraid to ask for help from someone more experienced in the area that we are needing help in.

When I first started in the business of becoming an Author, I did not know anything about anything. I did not even know that I would be an Author. After jotting things down and sharing my experiences, it seemed to be coming along as a story that could possibly be a book. It was at this point, that I began connecting with other writers and joining writer's groups etc. to gain the knowledge and expertise of those who had spent years in the field, and who could possibly teach me how to polish my own craft. So I educated myself. I also began to **Explore** those qualities that I already had, and worked to sharpen my skills in those areas. We all have our own set of unique gifts and we all have an audience out there waiting for us to discover our gifts so that we can share them with the world.

P=**Potential**- Do something that you have been afraid to do. It may be going LIVE on Facebook, doing your own Podcast, taking swimming lessons, whatever the case may be. What this will do, is help you to overcome fear and build your confidence to do things that you may consider new or beyond your ability to do. This year, we are overcoming some stuff. Everything that you need to strategize and shift your thinking so that you can SOAR into your next level is already inside of you. You have to find this place in you and tap into it. When you find it and embrace it, STEPPING will be a thing of old, you will float through life ripe, ready, free, and equipped to change the universe with messages and testimonials of hope and inspiration. The sky is the limit or is it? When we think about STEPPING, we think about confronting or approaching something or someone. What is it, or who is it that you need to confront or approach that has been preventing you from moving forward? Forgiving sets us free. To be free to STEP forward in God's will or life in general, we must be ready and willing to forgive others their trespasses against us. God wants you to have all that He says you can, but unforgiveness in your heart will hold you back and empower the other person. When you forgive, it not only releases the other person's hold on your life, it frees you to do all that you would have done, if you had not allowed this person to steal your joy. Take back your life and STEP into God's best for you today!

Teresa A. Stith

Forgiving
Sets
You
Free

In a Women's Meeting one night, I was rather shocked when myself and my Christian Sisters were asked to draw names. Whoever name we chose, we were to go to the Bible and find a woman that we thought that particular Sister resembled in likeness.

Here's what one Sister wrote to me:

Sister Teresa- Hagar (The Woman who lost a bottle but **found a well**) Genesis 16; 21:9-17; 25:12; Galatians 24-25.

"As I read about Hagar, I saw Sister Teresa. Sometimes we lose focus because we have lost something so dear to us, or something that we think can save our lives, but we never look to see what is that greater thing that God has for us. If you would just call on Him and cry out to Him, He will hear you. Hagar thought that the bottle of water would keep her and her son.

How small-minded we can be when it comes to Christ and the wonders of His works, or rather how we look to see the smaller object instead of the bigger, more bountiful picture that God has placed in front of us. God's grace is covering you, understand His purpose for you."

Wow! In order for us to STEP, we have to be willing to see beyond our physical locations. We have to be able to trust God beyond our natural ability to do so. To do that, you must be connected to Him in a way that the world is not. This is through RELATIONSHIP.

About The Author

Teresa Ann Stith was born and raised in Brunswick County, Virginia. Her life experiences, hardships, and struggles have allowed her to have an overwhelming need and passion to motivate and inspire any and everyone who faces adversity. She is a motivator, a teacher and instructor in righteousness. She loves the Lord.

STEP is her fourth title in 2 years and she thanks God for His grace and mercy in allowing her to be able to speak to the nations through her writings about her own personal experiences that have drawn her closer to the Lord and taught her how to have a relationship with the Father. She is honored and humbled to see how God has fulfilled every promise spoken to her. She urges her audiences to keep the faith, despise not the day of small beginnings, and do not be afraid to STEP!

Have not I commanded thee?

Be strong and of a good courage;

be not afraid, neither be thou dismayed:

for the Lord thy God is with thee

whithersoever thou goest.

Joshua 1:9

Check out these other titles by "yours truly" and rejoice as you dig deep and discover new strengths and skills that you have, that have laid dormant in you for years. It's time to work that thing in you that will bring you the ultimate joy!

Remember, book reviews are important. Write your review of the book on Amazon at...
https://amazon.com/author/teresastith

Visit my online store at...

https://faith-it-to-make-it.myshopify.com

Find me on Facebook at... Afaiththatworks

Visit my website at...

https://www.afaiththatworks.com

Thank you for all of your prayers and support of this ministry. God bless each of you!

Made in the USA
Middletown, DE
18 April 2022